D1710283

Team Spirit

THE DENVER NUGGETS

BY

MARK STEWART

Content Consultant
Matt Zeysing
Historian and Archivist
The Naismith Memorial Basketball Hall of Fame

NORWOOD HOUSE PRESS

CHICAGO, ILLINOIS

Norwood House Press
P.O. Box 316598
Chicago, Illinois 60631

For information regarding Norwood House Press, please visit our website at:
www.norwoodhousepress.com or call 866-565-2900.

All photos courtesy of Getty Images except the following:
Denver Rockets (6), Topps, Inc. (7, 9, 14, 20, 21, 28, 29, 36, 40 top & bottom left, 43),
The Upper Deck Company/Author's Collection (30), Author's Collection (34, 40 bottom),
The Star Co. (39), Matt Richman (48).
Cover Photo: Steve Yeater/AP Images
Special thanks to Topps, Inc.

Editor: Mike Kennedy
Designer: Ron Jaffe
Project Management: Black Book Partners, LLC.
Research: Joshua Zaffos

Special thanks to Ellen Fliegelman, Sarah Hatfield, and Marty Fliegelman

Library of Congress Cataloging-in-Publication Data

Stewart, Mark, 1960-
  The Denver Nuggets / by Mark Stewart ; content consultant, Matt Zeysing.
    p. cm. -- (Team spirit)
  Includes bibliographical references and index.
  Summary: "Presents the history and accomplishments of the Denver
Nuggets basketball team. Includes highlights of players, coaches, and awards,
quotes, timelines, maps, glossary and websites"--Provided by publisher.
  ISBN-13: 978-1-59953-289-9 (library edition : alk. paper)
  ISBN-10: 1-59953-289-1 (library edition : alk. paper) 1. Denver Nuggets
(Basketball team)--History--Juvenile literature. I. Zeysing, Matt. II.
Title.
  GV885.52.D46S84 2009
  796.323'640978883--dc22
                                              2008039807

Manufactured in the United States of America.

COVER PHOTO: The Nuggets celebrate a win during the 2007–08 season.

Table of Contents

SPORTS WORDS & VOCABULARY WORDS: In this book, you will find many words that are new to you. You may also see familiar words used in new ways. The glossary on page 46 gives the meanings of basketball words, as well as "everyday" words that have special basketball meanings. These words appear in **bold type** throughout the book. The glossary on page 47 gives the meanings of vocabulary words that are not related to basketball. They appear in ***bold italic type*** throughout the book.

BASKETBALL SEASONS: Because each basketball season begins late in one year and ends early in the next, seasons are not named after years. Instead, they are written out as two years separated by a dash, for example 1944–45 or 2005–06.

Meet the Nuggets

Nothing is more fun than watching a high-scoring basketball game. The Denver Nuggets know this better than anyone. They have been lighting up the scoreboard—and putting smiles on fans' faces—for more than 40 seasons.

The Nuggets have been part of the sporting scene in Denver, Colorado since the 1960s. Year in and year out, they treat their fans to quick-thinking, fast-moving, and high-flying basketball. This style of play has become the "calling card" of the Nuggets. Sometimes they win, and sometimes they lose—but they never miss a chance to thrill the crowd.

This book tells the story of the Nuggets. They look for players with talent and heart. They encourage those players to have fun and be creative. When a player pulls on a Denver jersey, he knows it is time to put on a show. That is why every Nuggets game is truly a celebration of basketball.

Kenyon Martin and Carmelo Anthony celebrate a good play during a 2007–08 game.

Way Back When

T he Nuggets have played in Denver since 1967. That year the team was part of the new **American Basketball Association (ABA)**. The ABA started as a *rival* to the older **National Basketball Association (NBA)**. Back then, the team had a different name. They were called the Rockets.

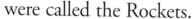

The Rockets had several good players in their early years. Larry Jones was one of the best **all-around** guards in basketball. Byron Beck was a rough-and-tumble forward. In 1969, 20-year-old Spencer Haywood joined the team. He led the ABA in points, rebounds, and minutes played as a **rookie**. Haywood left the club after one season for the NBA. Denver fans were very disappointed.

In 1974, the Rockets became the Nuggets. The people who ran the team hoped to join the NBA one day. The league already had a team called the Rockets, so Denver changed its name. The Nuggets had some excellent players during the 1970s, including Ralph Simpson, Dave Robisch, Julius Keye, Mack Calvin, Warren Jabali, Marvin Webster, Bobby Jones, and Dan Issel.

Denver's best player was David Thompson. He joined the team for the 1975–76 season. Thompson was the top pick in the **NBA draft**. He chose the Nuggets over the Atlanta Hawks. It was the first time in nine years that the top pick signed with an ABA team. This changed the way many people viewed the league. Thompson was a great shooter and defender—and an amazing leaper. He led Denver to the **ABA Finals** as a rookie.

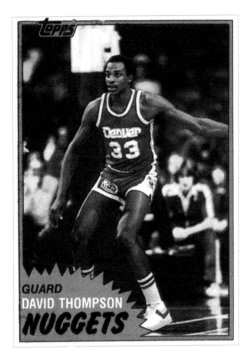

After the season, the ABA went out of business. The Nuggets were one of four teams invited to join the NBA. Denver fans wondered how the team would do in the older league. They were thrilled by the results. Thompson and Issel often scored 50 points or more a game. That helped the Nuggets finish first in the **Midwest Division** twice in a row. In 1977–78, the team reached the **Western Conference Finals**. Denver lost to the Seattle Supersonics in six games.

During the 1980s, the Nuggets were known as a "run-and-gun" team. Their games were fun to watch, with lots of dunks and amazing

LEFT: Ralph Simpson shares the cover of Denver's 1973 yearbook with coach Alex Hannum.
ABOVE: David Thompson, one of the greatest players in team history.

passing. It was not unusual for the Nuggets to score 120 or more points a game. In fact, the 1981–82 team set a record by averaging 126.5 points per game.

Denver's leaders during that time were guard Lafayette "Fat" Lever and forwards Alex English and Kiki Vandeweghe. Denver finished in first or second place in its division five times during the **decade**. However, the team could not win a championship. The Nuggets reached the Western Conference Finals in the spring of 1985. Unfortunately, they lost to the Los Angeles Lakers.

The Nuggets fell on hard times in the 1990s. Despite having skilled players such as Dikembe Mutombo, Mahmoud Abdul-Rauf, and Antonio McDyess, they lost far more often than they won. The fans loved to see a wide-open style of basketball, and the players liked to see all the points next to their names at the end of a game. The problem was that Denver's opponents had learned to beat them at their own game.

For the Nuggets to win the NBA championship, they had to build a team that played tougher defense. As the new **century** began, Denver looked for new players to match this **strategy**.

LEFT: Alex English rises for a layup. He led the high-scoring Nuggets during the 1980s.   **ABOVE**: A trading card of Antonio McDyess.

The Team Today

In the early years of the 21st century, Denver fans asked themselves a question. Could a team find success in today's NBA playing the Nuggets' wide-open style of basketball? The answer was *Yes*. But Denver also focused on defense. Stopping opponents from scoring was necessary to become a championship **contender**.

The Nuggets **drafted** a young star named Carmelo Anthony and surrounded him with quality players such as Marcus Camby, Kenyon Martin, Nenê Hilario, and Andre Miller. They hired a new coach, George Karl, who brought a new attitude to the court. After Karl took over in the middle of the 2004–05 season, the Nuggets won 32 of their last 40 games!

The Nuggets took their division in 2005–06. The following season, they finished with 50 victories. In 2008–09, Chauncey Billups joined the team and provided valuable leadership from the backcourt. With the team back on the winning track, Denver fans were ready to take that final step and root for a champion.

Chauncey Billups and Carmelo Anthony go over their game plan during the 2008–09 season.

Home Court

The team's first home was the Denver Auditorium Arena. When it was built in the early 1900s, it was the second-largest sports arena in America. However, the building held fewer than 7,000 fans for basketball.

In 1975, the Nuggets moved into the McNichols Sports Arena. It held more than twice as many fans as the Denver Auditorium. The "Big Mac" was located next to Mile High Stadium, where the Broncos football team played.

In 1999, the Nuggets moved into another new arena. The NBA held the **All-Star Game** there in 2005. The team shares the building with the Colorado Avalanche hockey team. It was also the site of the 2008 *Democratic National Convention*.

BY THE NUMBERS

- *The Nuggets' arena has 19,309 seats for basketball.*
- *The arena covers 4.6 acres of land.*
- *As of 2008, the Nuggets had retired four uniform numbers—2 (Alex English), 33 (David Thompson), 40 (Byron Beck), and 44 (Dan Issel).*

Excited fans get ready for a 2008 playoff game in the Nuggets' arena.

Dressed for Success

The Nuggets have used many different uniform colors and *logos* over the years. In the early 1970s, the team logo was a rocket dribbling a basketball. Denver's colors were purple and gold.

In 1974, the Rockets became the Nuggets. Their logo changed to Maxie the Miner. He held a *pickaxe* in one hand and an ABA basketball in the other. The ball was meant to be a valuable nugget he had discovered. At this time, the Nuggets also started using blue and white as their main colors.

RALPH SIMPSON • G

During the 1980s, the team's uniform and logo showed the Rocky Mountains. Denver made the change because there are wonderful views of the mountains from every part of the city. In the 1990s, the mountains disappeared from the team's uniform. However, this backdrop is still a part of the Nuggets' logo. Since 2003, the team has used a color combination of light blue, white, and gold.

Ralph Simpson models the Denver uniform from the team's days in the ABA.

UNIFORM BASICS

The basketball uniform is very simple. It consists of a roomy top and baggy shorts.

- The top hangs from the shoulders, with big "scoops" for the arms and neck. This style has not changed much over the years.

- Shorts, however, have changed a lot. They used to be very short, so players could move their legs freely. In the last 20 years, shorts have actually gotten longer and much baggier.

Basketball uniforms look the same as they did long ago … until you look very closely. In the old days, the shorts had belts and buckles. The tops were made of a thick cotton called "jersey," which got very heavy when players sweated. Later, uniforms were made of shiny *satin*. They may have looked great, but they did not "breathe." Players got very hot! Today, most uniforms are made of *synthetic* materials that soak up sweat and keep the body cool.

Nenê Hilario lines up a free throw in the Nuggets' 2007–08 home uniform.

We Won!

The Nuggets have had some amazing teams over the years. However, their path to the championship was always blocked. Their first visit to the league finals came in the last ABA season. The Nuggets lost to the New York Nets in a thrilling series.

Denver's greatest victory in the **playoffs** came at the end of the 1993–94 season. Eight teams advanced to the **postseason** from the Western Conference. The Nuggets finished the year 42–40. That made them the eighth team, which meant they had to play the Seattle Supersonics. Seattle was the top team in the conference and had the NBA's best record. No one believed the Nuggets had a chance.

As underdogs go, the Nuggets were no ordinary team. They had the NBA's youngest squad, so they had lots of energy. Denver was led by Dikembe Mutombo, a long-armed center who loved to block shots. He was joined by two other big men, Brian Williams and LaPhonso Ellis. Coach Dan Issel told this trio of players that they needed to control the area around both baskets. Otherwise, the Nuggets would not be able to keep up with Seattle.

The Sonics won the first two games easily on their home court. Back then, it took only three victories to win a playoff series in the first

Dikembe Mutombo watches as teammate LaPhonso Ellis scores a basket during the 1993–94 season. The Nuggets needed big performances from both to beat the Seattle Supersonics.

round. That meant the Nuggets had their backs against the wall. Issel gave the team some good advice—you have nothing to lose, so relax and have fun.

The Nuggets won Game 3 by a score of 110–93. Three days later, they battled the Sonics into **overtime** and won 94–85. The fifth and final game of the series was scheduled for Seattle. The Sonics were super-confident. Their record at home that year was 39–4. They still did not take the Nuggets seriously.

The Sonics tried to make the young Nuggets nervous with a tough defensive effort. This plan did not work. Again and again, Denver broke through for easy baskets. The Nuggets got their big break when Gary Payton hurt his foot. Without their best player, the Sonics struggled to score. Denver, meanwhile, teamed up against Shawn Kemp, Seattle's other star. Kemp scored only six points in the second half.

By the time the Sonics realized they were in trouble, it was too late. Mutombo was blocking shots and ***dominating*** near the basket. Williams had 17 points and 19 rebounds. Robert Pack, a guard who usually sat on the bench, scored 23 points.

It took a desperate shot by the Sonics to tie the game at the end of the fourth quarter. The Nuggets continued to play well and won 98–94 in overtime. When the buzzer sounded to end the game, Mutombo clutched the basketball and fell to the ground. He could not contain his joy. The Nuggets had done the impossible—and made history at the same time.

George Karl was the coach of the shocked Seattle team. Later, he became the Nuggets' coach. "That's probably my most miserable moment and most miserable day of my life," he said later. "I really don't have any fond memories of it because there's always the flashback of Mutombo laying on the ground that comes in every package of highlights made."

LEFT: Mutombo swats away a shot by Detlef Schrempf of the Sonics during the 1994 playoffs.   **ABOVE**: LaPhonso Ellis and Brian Williams hug after Denver's emotional victory over Seattle.

Go-To Guys

To be a true star in the NBA, you need more than a great shot. You have to be a "go-to guy"—someone teammates trust to make the winning play when the seconds are ticking away in a big game. Fans of the Rockets and Nuggets have had a lot to cheer about over the years, including these great stars …

THE PIONEERS

BYRON BECK   6´ 9˝ Forward

ROCKETS
BYRON BECK

- BORN: 1/25/1945
- PLAYED FOR TEAM: 1967–68 TO 1976–77

Byron Beck played for Denver in all nine of the team's ABA years. He had a good hook shot and fought for every loose ball and rebound. His extra effort made him the team's leader.

LARRY JONES   6´ 2˝ Guard

- BORN: 9/22/1942
- PLAYED FOR TEAM: 1967–68 TO 1969–70

Larry Jones was one of the first ABA players to excel in all areas of basketball. Jones scored 52 points in a game in 1967–68. It was the most by any player in the first year of the ABA.

ABOVE: Byron Beck   **RIGHT**: Dan Issel

RALPH SIMPSON   6′ 5″ Guard/Forward

- BORN: 8/10/1949   • PLAYED FOR TEAM: 1970–71 TO 1975–76 & 1977–78

Ralph Simpson was what today's fans call a "swingman." He could play guard or forward. Simpson averaged nearly 20 points a game for Denver and played in the ABA All-Star Game five times.

BOBBY JONES   6′ 9″ Forward

- BORN: 12/18/1951   • PLAYED FOR TEAM: 1974–75 TO 1977–78

Bobby Jones might have been the best defensive player in the ABA. His long arms and quick thinking gave him an advantage over everyone he guarded. He was also a great leaper who could slam the ball over anyone.

DAVID THOMPSON   6′ 4″ Guard

- BORN: 7/13/1954   • PLAYED FOR TEAM: 1975–76 TO 1981–82

David Thompson was impossible to stop. He could shoot from anywhere on the court and jumped higher than every player he faced. Thompson was a great dunker, too. He could cradle the ball in one arm and then punch it down through the basket with his other hand!

DAN ISSEL   6′ 9″ Forward

- BORN: 10/25/1948
- PLAYED FOR TEAM: 1975–76 TO 1984–85

Dan Issel was nicknamed the "Horse" because of his size, speed, and *stamina*. He was an excellent shooter who did not mind diving on the floor for loose balls. Issel later coached the Nuggets to some of their greatest victories.

MODERN STARS

ALEX ENGLISH   6´ 7˝ Forward

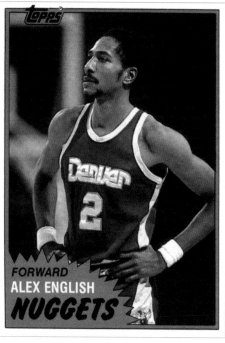

FORWARD
ALEX ENGLISH
NUGGETS

- BORN: 1/5/1954
- PLAYED FOR TEAM: 1979–80 TO 1989–90

The Nuggets were the perfect team for Alex English. He was at his best when the action was fast. English was quick and smooth, and a good shooter. He was Denver's highest scorer during the 1980s.

DIKEMBE MUTOMBO   7´ 2˝ Center

- BORN: 6/25/1966
- PLAYED FOR TEAM: 1991–92 TO 1995–96

Dikembe Mutombo was the best defensive center in the NBA when he played for the Nuggets. After blocking shots, he liked to wave his finger as if to say, "Don't try that again!" Mutombo was named the NBA's **Defensive Player of the Year** in his fourth season in Denver.

ANTONIO McDYESS   6´ 9˝ Forward

- BORN: 9/7/1974
- PLAYED FOR TEAM: 1995–96 TO 1996–97 & 1998–99 TO 2001–02

Antonio McDyess was a great leaper and an accurate shooter. In 1998–99, he became only the third Nugget to average 20 points and 10 rebounds a game in the same season. McDyess was a member of the U.S. *Olympic* basketball team that won a gold medal in 2000.

ABOVE: Alex English   **RIGHT**: Chauncey Billups

MARCUS CAMBY   6´ 11˝ Center/Forward

- BORN: 3/22/1974
- PLAYED FOR TEAM: 2002–03 TO 2007–08

The Nuggets traded for Marcus Camby to give the team a great defensive player. Camby used his long arms and quick reactions to block shots and grab rebounds. After the 2006-07 season, he was named the league's Defensive Player of the Year.

CARMELO ANTHONY   6´ 8˝ Forward

- BORN: 5/29/1984
- FIRST SEASON WITH TEAM: 2003–04

Denver drafted Carmelo Anthony after he led his college team to the national championship. In his rookie season, the Nuggets improved their record by 26 wins. In March of 2006, "Melo" became the second-youngest player in the NBA to reach 5,000 points.

CHAUNCEY BILLUPS   6´ 3˝ Guard

- BORN: 9/25/1976
- PLAYED FOR TEAM: 1998–99 TO 1999–00 & 2008–09 TO PRESENT

Chauncey Billups grew up in Colorado and also played college basketball in his home state. He dreamed of becoming the leader of the Nuggets but was traded away after two seasons with the team. When Denver had a chance to bring Billups back in 2008–09, the team didn't hesitate.

On the Sidelines

The Nuggets have had some of the finest coaches in basketball history work on their sidelines. One of the best was Larry Brown. Before becoming the team's coach, he played one year for Denver and set a club record with 23 **assists** in a game. Brown returned to coach the Nuggets and led them to the ABA Finals. Brown also guided the team to two division titles in the NBA. He taught the Nuggets that good defense was the key to winning close games.

Doug Moe, who was Brown's boyhood friend and ABA teammate, also coached the Nuggets. During the 1980s, Moe helped make them the highest-scoring team in the NBA. The Nuggets loved playing his fast-paced style. It meant more shots for everyone!

The team hired George Karl in the middle of the 2004–05 season. The Nuggets were unhappy with their 17–25 record. Under Karl, they finished the season strong and made the playoffs. In 2006, Karl became only the 12th NBA coach ever to win 800 games.

George Karl and Doug Moe watch the action from the bench. After Karl took over as the Nuggets' coach, he asked Moe to return to Denver and be an assistant.

One Great Day

When you buy a ticket for the last game of a season, you hope that the contest will be important. That didn't seem to be the case when the Nuggets faced the Detroit Pistons in the last game of the 1977–78 season. Denver had already won the Midwest Division. Detroit would not make the playoffs.

The game, however, meant everything to Denver's David Thompson. He and George Gervin of the San Antonio Spurs were neck-and-neck for the league scoring championship. With one game to go, Gervin had a slight lead. That afternoon, the Nuggets passed Thompson the ball whenever they could. The Pistons were helpless to stop him.

Thompson made 28 of 38 shots and poured in 73 points. When the game ended, his scoring average stood at 27.15 points per game. He also broke a record for most points in a quarter with 32 in the first period. Wilt Chamberlain had held the mark since 1962.

The Spurs played their last game that night. When Gervin heard about Thompson's amazing performance, he did some quick math. He

David Thompson soars toward the basket during the 1977–78 season.
He barely lost the scoring title to George Gervin that year.

knew he had to score at least 58 points to pass Thompson. The Spurs kept feeding Gervin the ball, and he kept shooting—until he had 63 points. He won the scoring championship with an average of 27.22. Along the way, Gervin scored 33 points in the second quarter.

Thompson was hardly disappointed afterward. He knew he had done his best. "It took me sixteen years to break Wilt's mark," Thompson joked. "It only took Gervin seven hours to break mine!"

Legend Has It

BOBBY JONES • F

Which ABA team was the toughest to beat at home?

LEGEND HAS IT that the Nuggets were. In the mid-1970s, basketball fans packed the team's arena. Visiting players were not used to such a large and noisy crowd. The Nuggets used this to their advantage. During the 1975–76 season, they won 28 home games in a row. When the Nuggets joined the NBA, even more fans came to see them. In 1976–77, they averaged 17,150 fans per game—the highest number in all of basketball.

ABOVE: Bobby Jones, one of the stars who made the Nuggets nearly impossible to beat on the home court. **RIGHT**: Dikembe Mutombo, whose full name took a long time to pronounce.

Who had the NBA's longest name?

LEGEND HAS IT that Dikembe Mutombo did. He was born in the African nation of Zaire. His full name is Dikembe Mutombo Mpolondo Mukamba Jean Jacque Wamutombo. Mutombo also spoke more languages than anyone in the league. He could speak English, French, Portuguese, Spanish, and at least five African languages.

Why was Denver's team originally named the Rockets?

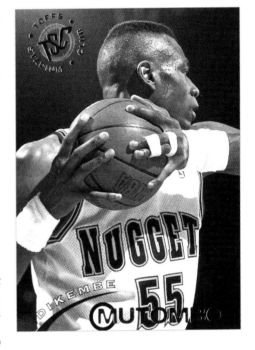

LEGEND HAS IT that they were named after a truck company. Bill Ringsby, the team's owner, also owned Rocket Truck Lines. The name was good for Denver because many aerospace companies were located there. Legend also has it that Dennis Murphy, who helped start the ABA, wanted to call the team the Lark Buntings after Colorado's state bird!

It Really Happened

During the 1960s, NBA teams refused to go after a player who was still a college student. When the ABA decided to play by its own rules, the Denver Rockets led the way.

Many people at the time thought the NBA policy was unfair. Some college players came from poor families and needed to make money. These young stars understood that a good education was important. But they knew it was more important to take care of their loved ones.

Four years was a long time to wait to start an NBA career.

By drafting young college players, the ABA could solve the "hardship" problem that many players faced. The league saw another advantage. It could also beat the NBA in the race to find the best basketball talent.

Spencer Haywood was the first "hardship player" ever signed by the ABA. He became a member of the Rockets at the age of twenty. Haywood had been the star of the U.S. men's basketball team during the 1968 Olympics. The teenager thought about going pro during his sophomore season in college.

Haywood was like no other player in the ABA. He had a smooth shot, quick hands and feet, and good jumping ability. The 6′ 8″ forward could run up and down the court all game, while other players huffed and puffed. Haywood made scoring and rebounding look so easy that even his teammates were amazed.

Within a few weeks of joining the ABA, Haywood had become one of the league's best players. He was named the top player in the All-Star Game. Haywood led the ABA in scoring and rebounding. At the end of the year, he was voted the **Rookie of the Year** and **Most Valuable Player (MVP)**.

Unfortunately for fans in Denver, Haywood left the Rockets after one spectacular season. He signed a new contract for more money with the Seattle Supersonics of the NBA. In 1971, a court ruled that the NBA's "four-year rule" was unfair. Haywood and all college basketball players were now free to go **pro** whenever they wanted.

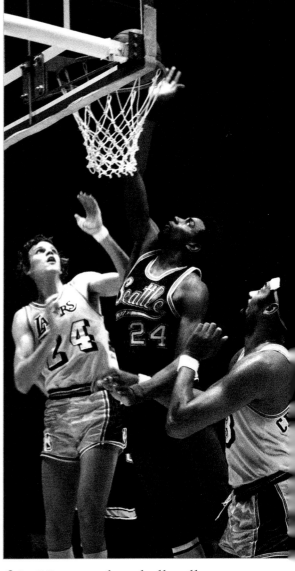

LEFT: A trading card shows Spencer Haywood with his All-Star Game MVP trophy.   **ABOVE**: Haywood battles for a rebound as a member of the Seattle Supersonics.

Saturday, April 19
7:30pm vs. S.J. EARTHQUAKES

RAPIDS HOME GAME
Dick's Sporting Goods Park

Team Spirit

Basketball has a long history in Denver. For many years, the Amateur Athletic Union (AAU) held its basketball championship in the city. Fans got to see the best players in the world compete. In the early years of the NBA, another pro team called the Nuggets played in Denver. They were part of the league for one year before going out of business.

Denver was a football town when today's Nuggets arrived. That changed in the mid-1970s. Nuggets fans were among the most loyal in basketball during that period. The team rewarded them with exciting teams and high-scoring games. No arena was noisier than Denver's when the Nuggets were racing up and down the court and rolling up a big score.

Now the cheering never seems to stop. During timeouts, the Nuggets Dancers and Nuggets Cheer Team entertain the crowd. The Nuggets often have other surprises for the fans, too. The one visitor they can count on every game is Rocky. He is the club's slam-dunking mountain lion *mascot*.

Rocky finds fun ways to entertain fans during every Nuggets home game.

Timeline

The basketball season is played from October through June. That means each season takes place at the end of one year and the beginning of the next. In this timeline, the accomplishments of the Rockets and Nuggets are shown by season.

1967–68
The team goes 45–33 in its first season.

1976–77
The Nuggets join the NBA.

1969–70
Spencer Haywood wins the ABA MVP award.

1974–75
The team changes its name to the Nuggets.

1982–83
Alex English and Kiki Vandeweghe finish first and second in the NBA scoring race.

A bumper sticker from the team's early days when it was known as the Rockets.

LeBron James guards Carmelo Anthony during the 2008 All-Star Game.

1987–88
Doug Moe is named **Coach of the Year**.

1993–94
Dikembe Mutombo leads the NBA in blocked shots.

2007–08
Carmelo Anthony is voted to the starting lineup in the All-Star Game.

1986–87
Fat Lever leads the Nuggets in assists and rebounds.

2003–04
Voshon Lenard wins the NBA **3-Point** Shootout.

2008–09
The Nuggets play the Phoenix Suns in an outdoor game.

Fat Lever

Voshon Lenard holds his trophy as the 3-point champ.

Fun Facts

FAT FARM

Two of Denver's greatest players were Roland "Fatty" Taylor and Lafayette "Fat" Lever. Taylor was one of the ABA's best defensive players. Lever was a very good scorer and passer.

MOVING VICTORY

Mahmoud Abdul-Rauf joined the Nuggets in 1990. He overcame *Tourette Syndrome* to become an NBA star. Twice with Denver, he led the league in free throw shooting.

A SLAMMIN' PARTY

The most famous day in the ABA took place in Denver's McNichols Arena in 1976. The All-Star Game that year featured the first Slam Dunk Contest. David Thompson showed his "Rock the Cradle" slam for the first time. Julius Erving won the contest by taking off from the foul line for a dunk.

BLOCK PARTY

Dikembe Mutombo and Julius Keye share the team record for blocked shots in a game with 12. During a seven-game playoff series, Mutombo once swatted 38 shots!

TRIPLE DIGITS

In 1981–82, the Nuggets scored 100 points or more in each of their 82 games. No team had ever done that before.

YOU GO, GIRL

Ralph Simpson was known for his smooth shooting with the Nuggets. His daughter is known for her smooth singing. India.Arie is a famous jazz and soul musician who won two **Grammy Awards** in 2003.

THE SKY'S THE LIMIT

In 2008, the Nuggets played the Phoenix Suns in a **pre-season** game held outdoors. It was the first time since 1972 that NBA teams played in the open air.

LEFT: Mahmoud Abdul-Rauf
ABOVE: Dikembe Mutombo denies another scoring opportunity.

Talking Hoops

"When I wore shorts and gym shoes to work, the sky was the limit for me."

—*David Thompson, who was nicknamed "Skywalker"*

"All great teams have two things in common—defense and rebounding."

—*Larry Brown, on the secret of the Nuggets' success in the 1970s*

"Bringing in … Larry Brown probably saved the Denver **franchise**—and was the reason it was strong enough to get into the NBA two years later."

—*Dave Robisch, on how the team survived when the ABA went out of business*

"I cared what the fans thought about me, and I tried very hard to please them."

—Dan Issel, on what made him one of the all-time favorite Nuggets

"Our players can do anything they want to if they get open."

—Doug Moe, on the team's strategy in the 1980s

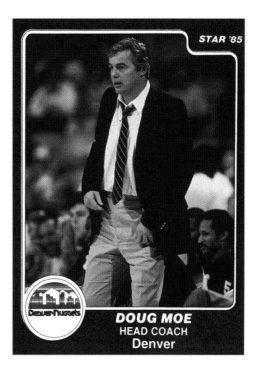

STAR '85

DOUG MOE
HEAD COACH
Denver

"I've never seen a player work as hard as he does."

—Scott Hastings, on teammate Dikembe Mutombo

"I'm coming home. To play in front of my family and friends, it makes me extremely happy."

—Chauncey Billups, on returning to Denver and the Nuggets

"Nobody should expect more of you than you expect of yourself."

—Carmelo Anthony, on how he motivates himself to get better each season

LEFT: David Thompson shows how he got the nickname "Skywalker."
ABOVE: Doug Moe

For the Record

The great Rockets and Nuggets teams and players have left their marks on the record books. These are the "best of the best" …

David Thompson

Dikembe Mutombo

NUGGETS AWARD WINNERS

WINNER	AWARD	SEASON
Spencer Haywood	ABA All-Star Game MVP	1969–70
Spencer Haywood	ABA Rookie of the Year	1969–70
Spencer Haywood	ABA Most Valuable Player	1969–70
Joe Belmont	ABA co-Coach of the Year	1969–70
Warren Jabali	ABA All-Star Game MVP	1972–73
Larry Brown	ABA Coach of the Year	1974–75
David Thompson	ABA All-Star Game MVP	1975–76
David Thompson	ABA Rookie of the Year	1975–76
Larry Brown	ABA Coach of the Year	1975–76
David Thompson	NBA All-Star Game MVP	1978–79
Doug Moe	NBA Coach of the Year	1987–88
Dikembe Mutombo	NBA Defensive Player of the Year	1994–95
Voshon Lenard	3-Point Shootout Champion	2003–04
Marcus Camby	NBA Defensive Player of the Year	2006–07

A Nuggets pennant from the 1970s.

NUGGETS ACHIEVEMENTS

ACHIEVEMENT	SEASON
ABA West Champions	1969–70
ABA West Champions	1974–75
NBA Midwest Champions	1976–77
NBA Midwest Champions	1977–78
NBA Midwest Champions	1984–85
NBA Midwest Champions	1987–88
NBA Northwest Champions	2005–06

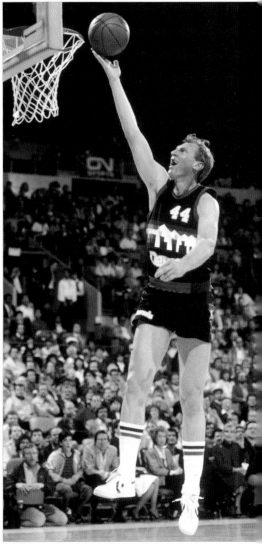

LEFT: Marcus Camby raises his trophy as the NBA's top defensive player in 2006–07.
ABOVE: Dan Issel, one of the leaders of the Nuggets during the 1970s and 1980s.

Pinpoints

The history of a basketball team is made up of many smaller stories. These stories take place all over the map—not just in the city a team calls "home." Match the push-pins on these maps to the Team Facts and you will begin to see the story of the Nuggets unfold!

TEAM FACTS

1 Denver, Colorado—*The team has played here since the 1967–68 season.*

2 Ellensburg, Washington—*Byron Beck was born here.*

3 Batavia, Illinois—*Dan Issel was born here.*

4 Detroit, Michigan—*Ralph Simpson was born here.*

5 Cincinnati, Ohio—*Dave Robisch was born here.*

6 Brooklyn, New York—*Carmelo Anthony was born here.*

7 Columbia, South Carolina—*Alex English was born here.*

8 Quitman, Mississippi—*Antonio McDyess was born here.*

9 Pine Bluff, Arkansas—*Fat Lever was born here.*

10 Sao Carlos, Brazil—*Nenê Hilario was born here.*

11 Wiesbaden, Germany—*Kiki Vandeweghe was born here.*

12 Kinshasa, Zaire*—*Dikembe Mutombo was born here.*

* This country is now the Democratic Republic of the Congo.

Dave Robisch

Play Ball

Basketball is a sport played by two teams of five players. NBA games have four 12-minute quarters—48 minutes in all—and the team that scores the most points when time has run out is the winner. Most baskets count for two points. Players who make shots from beyond the three-point line receive an extra point. Baskets made from the free-throw line count for one point. Free throws are penalty shots awarded to a team, usually after an opponent has committed a foul. A foul is called when one player makes hard contact with another.

Players can move around all they want, but the player with the ball cannot. He must bounce the ball with one hand or the other (but never both) in order to go from one part of the court to another. As long as he keeps "dribbling," he can keep moving.

In the NBA, teams must attempt a shot every 24 seconds, so there is little time to waste. The job of the defense is to make it as difficult as possible to take a good shot—and to grab the ball if the other team shoots and misses.

This may sound simple, but anyone who has played the game knows that basketball can be very complicated. Every player on the court has a job to do. Different players have different strengths and weaknesses. The coach must mix these players in just the right way, and teach them to work together as one.

The more you play and watch basketball, the more "little things" you are likely to notice. The next time you are at a game, look for these plays:

PLAY LIST

ALLEY-OOP—A play where the passer throws the ball just to the side of the rim—so a teammate can catch it and dunk in one motion.

BACK-DOOR PLAY—A play where the passer waits for his teammate to fake the defender away from the basket—then throws him the ball when he cuts back toward the basket.

KICK-OUT—A play where the ball-handler waits for the defense to surround him—then quickly passes to a teammate who is open for an outside shot. The ball is not really kicked in this play; the term comes from the action of pinball machines.

NO-LOOK PASS—A play where the passer fools a defender (with his eyes) into covering one teammate—then suddenly passes to another without looking.

PICK-AND-ROLL—A play where one teammate blocks or "picks off" another's defender with his body—then cuts to the basket for a pass in the confusion.

Glossary

BASKETBALL WORDS TO KNOW

3-POINT—A basket made from behind the 3-point line.

ABA FINALS—The playoff series that decides the champion of the league.

ALL-AROUND—Good at all parts of the game.

ALL-STAR GAME—The annual game in which the best players from the East and the West play against each other. The game does not count in the standings.

AMERICAN BASKETBALL ASSOCIATION (ABA)—The basketball league that played for nine seasons starting in 1967. Prior to the 1976–77 season, four ABA teams joined the NBA, and the rest went out of business.

ASSISTS—Passes that lead to successful shots.

COACH OF THE YEAR—The award given each season to the league's best coach.

DEFENSIVE PLAYER OF THE YEAR—The award given each year to the league's best defensive player.

DRAFTED—Chosen from a group of the best college players. The NBA draft is held each summer.

FRANCHISE—The players, coaches, and business people who make up a team.

MIDWEST DIVISION—The division for teams that play in the central part of the country.

MOST VALUABLE PLAYER (MVP)—The award given each year to the league's best player; also given to the best player in the league finals and All-Star Game.

NATIONAL BASKETBALL ASSOCIATION (NBA)—The professional league that has been operating since 1946–47.

NBA DRAFT—The annual meeting where teams pick from a group of the best college players.

OVERTIME—The extra period or periods played when a game is tied after 48 minutes.

PLAYOFFS—The games played after the season to determine the league champion.

POSTSEASON—Another term for playoffs.

PRE-SEASON—The practice games played before a season starts.

PRO—A player or team that plays a sport for money.

ROOKIE—A player in his first season.

ROOKIE OF THE YEAR—The annual award given to the league's best first-year player.

WESTERN CONFERENCE FINALS—The playoff series that determines which team from the West will play the best team in the East for the NBA Championship.

OTHER WORDS TO KNOW

CENTURY—A period of 100 years.

CONTENDER—A team that competes for a championship.

DECADE—A period of 10 years; also specific periods, such as the 1950s.

DEMOCRATIC NATIONAL CONVENTION—The national meeting where the Democratic party chooses its presidential candidate.

DOMINATING—Completely controlling through the use of power.

GRAMMY AWARDS—Honors given to people in the music industry.

LOGOS—Symbols or designs that represent a company or team.

MASCOT—An animal or person believed to bring a group good luck.

OLYMPIC—Describing the international sports competition held every four years.

PICKAXE—A tool used for digging and cutting.

RIVAL—Extremely emotional competitor.

SATIN—A smooth, shiny fabric.

STAMINA—The ability to sustain a long physical effort.

STRATEGY—A plan or method for succeeding.

SYNTHETIC—Made in a laboratory, not in nature.

TOURETTE SYNDROME—A disorder that prevents a person from controlling physical movements or vocal sounds.

Places to Go

ON THE ROAD

DENVER NUGGETS
1000 Chopper Circle
Denver, Colorado 80204
(303) 405-1100

NAISMITH MEMORIAL BASKETBALL HALL OF FAME
1000 West Columbus Avenue
Springfield, Massachusetts 01105
(877) 4HOOPLA

ON THE WEB

THE NATIONAL BASKETBALL ASSOCIATION   www.nba.com
  • *Learn more about the league's teams, players, and history*

THE DENVER NUGGETS   www.nba.com/nuggets
  • *Learn more about the Nuggets*

THE BASKETBALL HALL OF FAME   www.hoophall.com
  • *Learn more about history's greatest players*

ON THE BOOKSHELF

To learn more about the sport of basketball, look for these books at your library or bookstore:

  • Hareas, John. *Basketball.* New York, New York: DK, 2005.

  • Hughes, Morgan. *Basketball.* Vero Beach, Florida: Rourke Publishing, 2005.

  • Thomas, Keltie. *How Basketball Works.* Berkeley, California: Maple Tree Press, distributed through Publishers Group West, 2005.

Index

The Team

MARK STEWART has written more than 20 books on basketball, and over 100 sports books for kids. He grew up in New York City during the 1960s rooting for the Knicks and Nets, and now takes his two daughters, Mariah and Rachel, to watch them play. Mark comes from a family of writers. His grandfather was Sunday Editor of *The New York Times* and his mother was Articles Editor of *The Ladies Home Journal* and *McCall's*. Mark has profiled hundreds of athletes over the last 20 years. He has also written several books about his native New York, and New Jersey, his home today. Mark is a graduate of Duke University, with a degree in history. He lives with his daughters and wife, Sarah, overlooking Sandy Hook, New Jersey.

MATT ZEYSING is the resident historian at the Basketball Hall of Fame in Springfield, Massachusetts. His research interests include the origins of the game of basketball, the development of professional basketball in the first half of the twentieth century, and the culture and meaning of basketball in American society.